MISSISSIPPI

EXPLORE THE UNITED STATES ★ EXPLORE THE UNITED STATES ★ EXPLORE THE UNITED STATES ★ EXPLORE THE UNITED STATES

Julie

Big Buddy BOOKS

VISIT US AT
www.abdopublishing.com

Published by ABDO Publishing Company, PO Box 398166, Minneapolis, MN 55439.

Copyright © 2013 by Abdo Consulting Group, Inc. International copyrights reserved in all countries. No part of this book may be reproduced in any form without written permission from the publisher. Big Buddy Books™ is a trademark and logo of ABDO Publishing Company.

Printed in the United States of America, North Mankato, Minnesota.
042012
092012

 PRINTED ON RECYCLED PAPER

Coordinating Series Editor: Rochelle Baltzer
Editor: Sarah Tieck
Contributing Editors: Megan M. Gunderson, BreAnn Rumsch, Marcia Zappa
Graphic Design: Adam Craven
Cover Photograph: *Getty Images*: Adam Jones/Photo Researchers.
Interior Photographs/Illustrations: *Alamy*: ClassicStock (p. 9), Ian Dagnall (p. 5), Don Smetzer (p. 27) ; *AP Photo*: AP Photo (pp. 21, 23), Denis Farrell (p. 25), North Wind Picture Archives via AP Images (p. 13), PRNewsFoto/ Lieberman Management (p. 27), RogelioSolis (p. 21); *Getty Images*: STAN HONDA/AFP (p. 11), Matthew Sharpe (p. 26); *Glow Images*: Robert Harding (p. 29), Superstock (p. 19); *iStockphoto*: ©iStockphoto.com/ jondesign (p. 17), ©iStockphoto.com/pelicankate (pp. 26, 27); *Shutterstock*: Darryl Brooks (p. 30), Steve Byland (p. 30), eewill40 (p. 9), Phillip Lange (p. 30), BONNIE WATTON (p. 30).

All population figures taken from the 2010 US census.

Library of Congress Cataloging-in-Publication Data

Murray, Julie, 1969-
  Mississippi / Julie Murray.
    p. cm. -- (Explore the United States)
  ISBN 978-1-61783-362-5
  1. Mississippi--Juvenile literature. I. Title.
  F341.3.M873 2013
  976.2--dc23
                          2012007061

MISSISSIPPI

Contents

ONE NATION

The United States is a **diverse** country. It has farmland, cities, coasts, and mountains. Its people come from many different backgrounds. And, its history covers more than 200 years.

Today the country includes 50 states. Mississippi is one of these states. Let's learn more about this state and its story!

Did You Know?

Mississippi became a state on December 10, 1817. It was the twentieth state to join the nation.

The word *Mississippi* comes from a Native American word. It means "great waters" or "father of waters."

MISSISSIPPI UP CLOSE

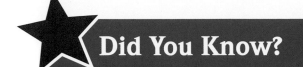
The United States has four main **regions**. Mississippi is in the South.

Mississippi has four states on its borders. Louisiana and Arkansas are west. Tennessee is north. Alabama is east. The Gulf of Mexico is south.

Mississippi has a total area of 47,692 square miles (123,522 sq km). About 3 million people live in the state.

REGIONS OF THE UNITED STATES

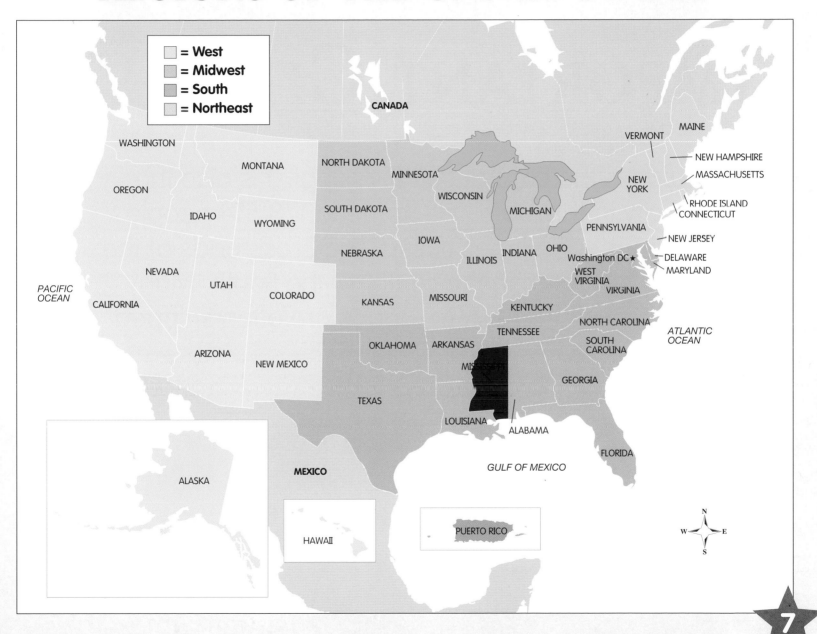

Map legend:
- = West
- = Midwest
- = South
- = Northeast

Important Cities

Jackson is the **capital** of Mississippi. It is also the largest city in the state. It is home to 173,514 people.

Jackson is sometimes called "the Crossroads of the South." It is located in the center of the South. Many businesses are there. Also, goods are often shipped through the city.

Downtown Jackson has businesses, restaurants, theaters, and museums.

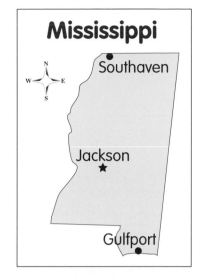

Mississippi

Southaven

Jackson

Gulfport

Jackson became the capital in 1822. The current state capitol building was completed in 1903.

Gulfport is the second-largest city in Mississippi. It is home to 67,793 people. This vacation area is on the Gulf of Mexico. It has many homes that date to the **American Civil War**.

Southaven is the state's third-largest city. It is home to 48,982 people. Its population grew by 69 percent between 2000 and 2010!

Mississippi in History

Mississippi's history includes Native Americans, farming, war, and the **civil rights movement**. Native Americans first lived on Mississippi's land. Later, Europeans settled there and began farming. Mississippi became a state in 1817.

By the 1830s, cotton had become a leading crop. **Slaves** worked cotton fields for landowners. After the **American Civil War**, they were freed.

In the 1950s, African Americans were still treated unfairly in Mississippi. The civil rights movement helped change things for the better.

In 1540, Hernando de Soto was the first European to explore Mississippi. He was looking for gold.

Many people were taken from Africa to work as slaves in the United States. Some were forced to work on large Mississippi farms.

Timeline

1848

The University of Mississippi opened in Oxford.

1861

Mississippi fought for the Southern states in the **American Civil War**.

1800s

Mississippi became the twentieth state on December 10.

1817

Insects called boll weevils destroyed Mississippi's cotton crop. Many families struggled to earn money. This hurt the state's economy.

1915

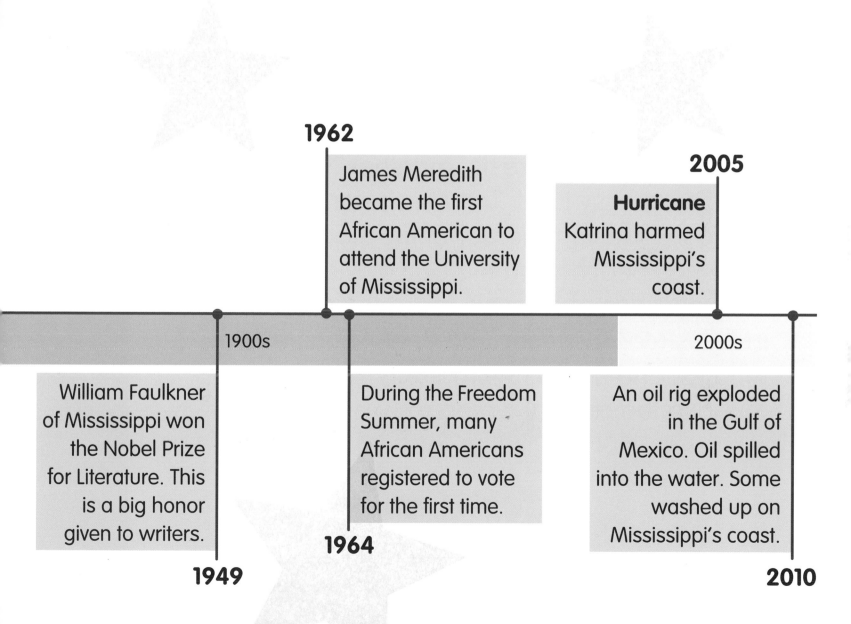

1962

James Meredith became the first African American to attend the University of Mississippi.

2005

Hurricane Katrina harmed Mississippi's coast.

1900s

2000s

William Faulkner of Mississippi won the Nobel Prize for Literature. This is a big honor given to writers.

During the Freedom Summer, many African Americans registered to vote for the first time.

An oil rig exploded in the Gulf of Mexico. Oil spilled into the water. Some washed up on Mississippi's coast.

1949

1964

2010

ACROSS THE LAND

Mississippi has forests, **marshes**, hills, coasts, and flat, grassy land. The Mississippi River flows along the western border of the state. And, the state has beaches on the Gulf of Mexico.

Many types of animals make their homes in this state. These include deer, rabbits, wild turkeys, and ducks. Shrimp and oysters are found in the coastal waters.

Did You Know?

In July, the average temperature in Mississippi is 81°F (27°C). In January, it is 46°F (8°C).

The Pearl River flows through
LeFleur's Bluff State Park in Jackson.

EARNING A LIVING

Manufacturing is an important business in Mississippi. Factories make furniture, car parts, food, and lumber.

Many people in the state work for the government. Government scientists test rockets at the Stennis Space Center near Bay Saint Louis.

Mississippi has large farms. Sweet potatoes, corn, and cotton are major crops. Catfish and chickens are also raised on farms.

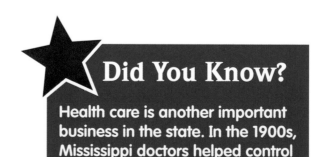

Did You Know?

Health care is another important business in the state. In the 1900s, Mississippi doctors helped control sicknesses such as yellow fever.

Some areas of Mississippi are warm enough for crops to grow almost all year.

SPORTS PAGE

College sports are popular in Mississippi. This includes football, basketball, and baseball. The University of Mississippi and Mississippi State University have talented football teams. They have been rivals for many years!

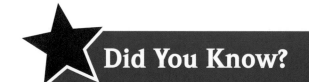

Did You Know?

Brett Favre was born in Gulfport. He played football for the University of Southern Mississippi. Later, he was a famous quarterback.

Archie Manning (*left*) and his son Eli (*above*) played football at the University of Mississippi. Both went on to become well-known quarterbacks.

HOMETOWN HEROES

Many famous people are from Mississippi. Elvis Presley was born in Tupelo in 1935.

Presley was a singer known as "the King of Rock and Roll." He is famous for hit rock songs. These include "Hound Dog," "Jailhouse Rock," and "All Shook Up."

Presley was also an actor. He appeared in more than 30 movies!

Presley starred in a movie called *Jailhouse Rock*. In it, he showed off his exciting dance moves.

23

Oprah Winfrey was born in Kosciusko in 1954. She is a famous talk-show host, actress, and businesswoman. She owns a magazine and a television network.

Winfrey hosted *The Oprah Winfrey Show* from 1985 to 2011. It was one of the most popular television shows ever.

★★★★★★★★★★★★★★★★★★★★★★★★★★★★★★★★★★★★

Winfrey is known for helping others. In 2007, she opened a school for girls in South Africa.

Tour Book

Do you want to go to Mississippi? If you visit the state, here are some places to go and things to do!

Remember

Take a boat to West Ship Island. There, you can see historic Fort Massachusetts. The building was started in the 1850s but was never finished.

Cheer

Attend a college football game. The University of Mississippi versus Mississippi State University games are known for being exciting!

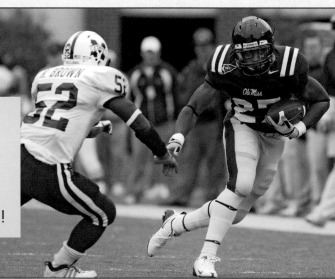

★ Listen

Take in some Mississippi Delta blues. This is a well-known style of music. Famous blues artist B.B. King (*left*) is from Mississippi.

★ See

Visit the Gulf Islands National Seashore. This string of small islands runs from Mississippi to Florida. It has salt marshes, forests, and beaches.

★ Discover

See huge stone logs in the Mississippi Petrified Forest. They used to be living trees. Some of the trees were once more than 100 feet (30 m) tall! Over millions of years, they turned to rock.

A GREAT STATE

The story of Mississippi is important to the United States. The people and places that make up this state offer something special to the country. Together with all the states, Mississippi helps make the United States great.

People swim, sail, and play at Biloxi's beaches on the Gulf of Mexico.

Fast Facts

Date of Statehood:
December 10, 1817

Population (rank):
2,967,297
(31st most-populated state)

Total Area (rank):
47,692 square miles
(31st largest state)

Motto:
"Virtute et Armis"
(By Valor and Arms)

Nickname:
Magnolia State

State Capital:
Jackson

Flag:

Flower: Southern Magnolia

Postal Abbreviation:
MS

Tree: Southern Magnolia

Bird: Northern Mockingbird

Important Words

American Civil War the war between the Northern and Southern states from 1861 to 1865.

capital a city where government leaders meet.

civil rights movement the public fight for civil rights for all citizens. Civil rights include the right to vote and freedom of speech.

diverse made up of things that are different from each other.

hurricane a tropical storm that forms over seawater with strong winds, rain, thunder, and lightning.

marsh an area of low, wet land.

region a large part of a country that is different from other parts.

slave a person who is bought and sold as property.

Web Sites

To learn more about Mississippi, visit ABDO Publishing Company online. Web sites about Mississippi are featured on our Book Links page. These links are routinely monitored and updated to provide the most current information available.

www.abdopublishing.com

Index